This journey belongs to:

_____

A collection of mindfulness exercises to guide doctoral students on a journey of peace & purpose throughout their studies

1st Edition

Danielle R Williams

*This journal is dedicated to the doctoral students who struggle with their mental health as a consequence of toxic academic culture.
I see you.*

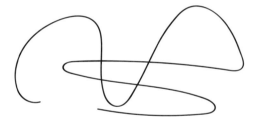

The Mindful PhD Journal 1st Edition
Copyright © 2022 by Danielle R. Williams

All rights reserved. No part of this publication may be reproduced or transmitted in any form or by any means without written permission from the copyright holders, except in the case of brief excerpts or quotes embedded in reviews, critical essays, or promotional materials where full credit is given to the copyright holder.

Limit of Liability/ Disclaimer of Warranty: The publisher/author make no representations or warranties with respect to the accuracy or completeness of the contents of this work and specifically disclaim all warranties, including without limitation warranties of fitness for a particular purpose. No warranty may be created or extended by sales or promotional materials. The advice and strategies contained herein may not be suitable for every situation. This work is sold with the understanding that the publisher is not engaged in rendering medical, legal, or other professional advice or services. If professional assistance is required, the services of a competent professional person should be sought. Neither the publisher/author shall be liable for damages arising herefrom. The fact that an individual, organization, institution, or website is referred to in this work as a citation and/or potential source of further information does not mean that the publisher/author endorses the information the individual, organization, or website may provide or recommendations they/it may make. Further, readers should be aware that websites listed in this work may have changed or disappeared between when this work was written and when it is read. For general information you may contact Infinite Gratitude, LLC at infinitegraditude.com

ISBN: 979-8-9857405-0-9

Published in the United States of America

Interior & Cover design: Danielle R. Williams
Art credits: Envato Market
Editor: JessieAnn D'Amico & Catherine Lewis
Author photo courtesy of Johnathan Robertson

CONTENTS

A letter from the author   9

Introduction to Mindfulness   13

Personal Reflection   17

The Self-work   62

Academic Perception   112

Final Thoughts   179

Resources   180

References   182

"

What you are is what you have been.
What you'll be is what you'll do now

-Buddha

A letter from the author

Imagine life as a graduate student. You plan ahead to manage your time efficiently. You have outlined the steps necessary to achieve each goal you've set. When moments of stress do arise, you have a tool kit of healthy coping mechanisms to ease those feelings. Your workload does not overwhelm you. In fact, you are at peace with an incomplete to-do list because you know your ultimate purpose and worth is not tied to your productivity. You are confident in guiding your own unique path to success as a graduate student. You know exactly why you are here.

How can you achieve this seemingly perfect experience as a graduate student? Mindfulness.

I'm originally from southeast San Diego, CA. I had my first encounter with the idea of mindfulness in 2015 when I took a Buddhist Psychology course with Dr. Lori Stewart at San Diego State University. I have carried The Wise Heart: A Guide to the Universal Teachings of Buddhist Psychology by Jack Kornfield with me ever since. Reading this book helped me heal from much of my childhood trauma, especially regarding my father passing when I was 12 years old. I am extremely grateful to have taken this class by happenstance. Finding The Wise Heart has forever changed my life.

I've been in academia for almost a decade, unfortunately becoming intimately familiar with how toxic academic work culture can be. The experience I had working as a post-baccalaureate researcher for two years stands out as a prominent example. As a first-generation, socioeconomically disadvantaged Black woman pursuing higher education in microbiology at a predominately white institution, to say I felt out of place is an understatement. I was told: "You're not ready for a PhD," "You should take undergraduate coursework instead of graduate-level coursework," "It doesn't even seem like you care," "You should apply to schools in the Midwest. They need Black people there," "If this is too much, you can choose a different route." These comments were all made while I worked 60 hours a week in lab (including weekends), worked a second job three days a week to manage debt from undergrad and the cost of living in Seattle, and took graduate level coursework to compensate for my extremely low (2.63) undergraduate GPA. It was my first time away from home, and I hit my breaking point when I got the news that my mother was ill in the hospital with pulmonary embolism and I couldn't even afford to go home.

I had lost much of the hope I arrived with. When my mental health declined to the point that it manifested physically – through nauseating migraines, lockjaw, hives, blackouts, and finally subconscious thoughts and dreams of suicide – I knew I had to get help.

I remembered the book from Jack Kornfield, pulled it off a shelf, and began to read. I'd been rereading the book for two days when a woman approached me on the bus. She said, "God wanted me to tell you, you are a light." Although I wasn't very religious at the time, my Christian upbringing led me to take this as confirmation that I was exactly where I needed to be.

Still, in the midst of the utter chaos of familial demands, schoolwork, and paying the bills, Jack Kornfield's book didn't provide the day-to-day structure I needed to receive and apply its wisdom.

So, I began therapy. This gave me order. It gave me hope. My therapist told me to get into a routine – to begin planning my days, to exercise more consistently, and to lean on the support of those around me. He recommended I get out of my toxic work environment.

He was right. I had had enough. I remember the day I staggered into Andrea's office, eyes welling with tears, heart pounding. She had been known to help students out of turbulent situations. But, if she didn't have a solution for me, I was ready to drop out of the program and never pursue academia again. Luckily, she had a solution. Within the month I had relocated to a different lab. I still get emotional when I think about the support, I received from the mentor who welcomed me into the lab. His belief in me ignited the light within me that had been dimmed for so long.

My new lab environment was wonderful. But I noticed I still held hatred and fear in my heart. Hatred that led me to begin self-sabotaging and doubting myself. Fear that fostered lingering anxiety and bouts of depression. I could not fully enjoy or be present for the new experience because I still hadn't healed from the previous one.

I realized that although my environment had changed, I had not.

I set out on the journey to build myself into someone who could grow within this new environment and get the most out of it. I began journaling consistently, pinpointing my triggers, deidentifying with my trauma of an unsupportive mentor and toxic work environment, and doing the self-work required to heal.

As I healed, I also became more consistent with the practical exercises my therapist had recommended. I prioritized my mental health and protected it at all costs. I knew I never wanted to experience that tumultuous mental state that had consumed me ever again.

This healing journey springboarded me into a journey of personal growth that has equppied me with tools to not only protect my mental health as a doctoral student but also to thrive in an academic setting.

This journal is a culmination of all the personal development exercises I've done to take back and hone my power.

I want you to know: despite institutional barriers and academic bureaucracy, you have full autonomy to guide your mental state to one of power, confidence, hopefulness, compassion, and gratitude. Journaling is a wonderful first step toward healing anxiety, fear, and depression.

Your personal growth journey and your academic journey are not mutually exclusive. In fact, integrating the two will bring more clarity and peace than you can imagine.

Here's to a Peaceful, Purposeful PhD,

Let's get started!

  Danielle

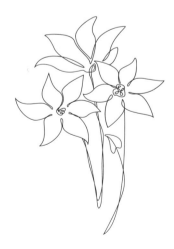

An Introduction to Mindfulness

Mindfulness originates from Buddhist practices dating back more than 25 centuries, but has recently gained traction in the Western Hemisphere infiltrating a number of disciplines[4,5]. It has been developed into various psychotherapy interventions such as acceptance and commitment therapy (ACT), mindfulness-based stress reduction (MBSR) and mindfulness-based cognitive therapy (MBCT).[7,9] Studies show these mindfulness interventions, are clearly related to well-being.[8] Many people associate mindfulness with meditation, and, although they go hand in hand, mindfulness also incorporates an attitude of curiosity, openness, and acceptance. It is not confined to meditation in the traditional sense but is to be applied throughout life – to listening, to eating, to every act and movement, to being.[9]

My favorite definition of mindfulness was very eloquently put by Dr. Jon Kabat-Zinn, a fellow molecular biologist, an emeritus professor at the University of Massachusetts Medical School, and also the creator of MBSR: "Paying attention in a particular way: on purpose, in the present moment, and non-judgmentally."[6]

Here are a few more definitions of mindfulness from various scholars:

Mindfulness is "paying attention to the present moment."[1,2]

"Mindfulness is the miracle by which we master and restore ourselves... awareness and non-judgmental acceptance of one's moment-to-moment experience."[9]

"It is inherently a state of consciousness which involves consciously attending to one's moment to moment experience."[3]

"Mindfulness practice is fundamentally simple: focus on the breath. Pay attention. Be aware."[10]

Components of Mindfulness

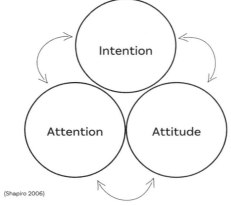

(Shapiro 2006)

Professor of Psychology, Shauna Shapiro, PhD breaks down mindfulness into an axiom that I love because it elaborates on Kabat-Zinn's original definition stated above. She specifies, "intention" translates to "on purpose," "paying attention" is "attention" and "in a particular way" refers to your "attitude"[3]. I have adapted a figure from her paper above to illustrate that the relationship between these aspects are interdependent and simultaneous.

More explicitly stated, being mindful "on purpose" requires some kind of personal vision.

This vision is often dynamic and always evolving.[6] It's been shown that as meditators continue to practice, they noticed that their intentions shift along a spectrum from self-regulation to self-exploration, and finally, self-liberation.[11] These phases were achieved solely based on the intentions they set. Alternatively stated, with deepening practice they were able to achieve greater awareness and insight as they shifted their goals and redefined their why.

The second axiom, "attention" is described as curative in and of itself. Paying attention to one's moment to moment experiences both internally and externally is crucial to the healing process.[6]

Attention improves one's ability to refrain from over processing thoughts and feelings and to be able to shift focus from unhealthy mental states to healthy mental states.[6]

Lastly, "attitude" refers to how we pay attention. Do we approach mindfulness with a bare critical lens or do we bring kindness, compassion, and an openhearted presence? Can we, in spite of aversive or unpleasant encounters, practice loving-kindness and acceptance? Being able to do so allows us to become non-judgmental of either positive or negative experiences, emotions, or thoughts. This how is the perspective of experience we apply to our mindfulness practice. Ultimately, we want to illuminate curiosity, non-striving, and acceptance in our awareness.[6]

The implications of mindfulness practices are notable because they target core processes such as increased emotional awareness and regulation, improved cognitive function, and goals-based behaviors[7,1]. As a result, mindfulness practice can be seen as an effective solution or treatment for psychological distress such as anxiety, worry, fear and anger. It also addresses tendencies to avoid, suppress, or overengage with one's distressing thoughts and emotions.[7]

The essence of the journal prompts in this book is centered around MBSR practices as defined by Dr. Kabat-Zinn. He articulates there are nine attitudes of mindfulness defined below[12]:

1. Non-judging: intentionally assume the perspective of an impartial witness
2. Patience: adopting a form of wisdom that accepts the fact that sometimes things must unfold in their own time
3. Beginner's Mind: a mind that is unassuming and is willing to see everything as if for the first time
4. Trust: developing a basic trust in the wisdom of your body and innate goodness
5. Non-striving: allowing things to be as they are without an expectation to change them
6. Acceptance: seeing things as they are and not for what you want them to be
7. Letting Go: intentionally release control and practice observing your experiences moment to moment
8. Gratitude: increasing your own experience of happiness
9. Generosity: graciously receiving from yourself and the universe

Keep these simplified definitions in mind as you voyage through this journal. The prompts and exercises within this journal serve as a guide to expose you to a new perspective that inspires hope, self-love, and opportunity.

Remember that mindfulness is a practice.

"What you practice grows stronger." -Shauna Shapiro

Personal Reflection
Deep introspection can cultivate purpose and fuel intense personal growth

Mindfulness Meditation

Breath Awareness

Set a timer for 5 minutes. Sit comfortably in a quiet space. Close your eyes. Bring your attention to the present moment by focusing on your breath. Pay attention to how your breath travels in and out of your body. During this time your mind may wander. This is perfectly okay. As it wanders become an observer of your own thoughts and feelings. Watch what is happening in your brain. Then gently allow yourself to return your attention to your breath.

While sitting in a quiet place, feelings of boredom or frustration may arise. Observe these as if you were a bystander. Accept them as they are. Likewise, observe and accept each thought or feeling that passes through your mind, then gently focus your attention back to your breath. Do this until your timer rings.

TherapistAid.com

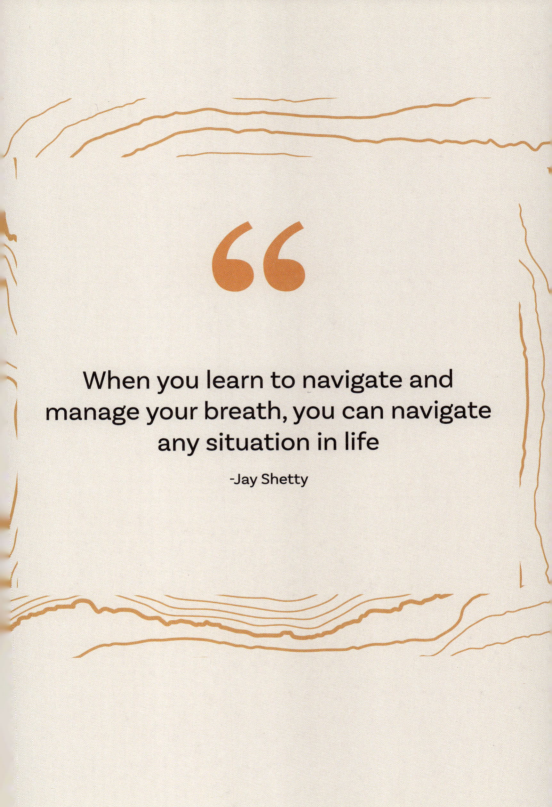

> When you learn to navigate and manage your breath, you can navigate any situation in life

-Jay Shetty

Write a list of 5 experiences you're grateful for.

Refer to your answer from the previous prompt. How did these experiences shape the person you are today?

Write a letter to your 10-year-old self. What advice would you offer?

Refer to the previous prompt. Have you implemented this advice? If so, how? If not, how do you think your life would be different as a result?

Affirmation

Say this aloud:

What I focus on, I magnify

Self-compassion

To have compassion means to empathize with someone who is suffering and to feel compelled to reduce their suffering.

When you exhibit self-compassion, you recognize your own suffering and take action to comfort and care for yourself. This recognition of suffering is without judgement and approached with an understanding that this is a natural part of being human.

When you are having a difficult time or notice a shortcoming, try acknowledging that whatever it is you're going through is really difficult and ask how you can comfort yourself in this moment.

TherapistAid.com

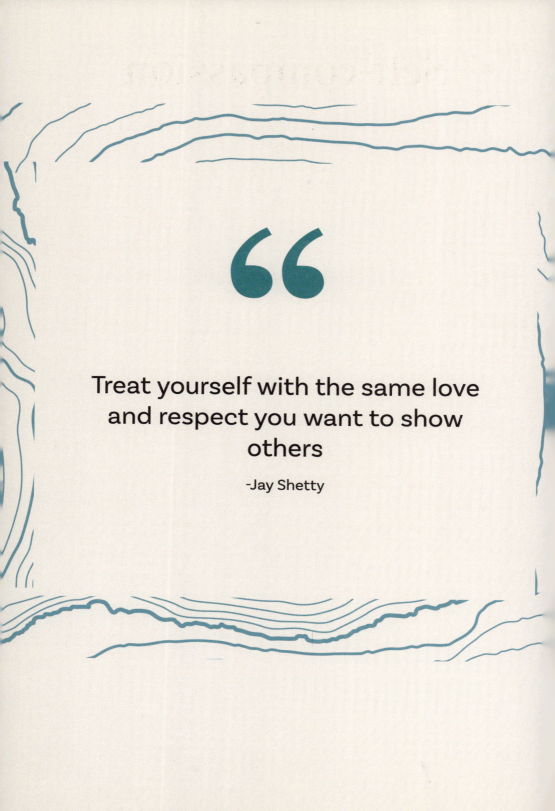

"

Treat yourself with the same love and respect you want to show others

-Jay Shetty

Write about a time when someone showed you an act of kindness. How did this make you feel?

Write about a time when you showed kindness to someone. How did this make you feel?

Write about a time when you showed yourself kindness. How does it make you feel to reflect on this?

"

When you change the way you look at things, the things you look at change

-Esther Hicks

Challenge Yourself

When you become aware of an experience where you fell short, take a moment to pause and focus on your breath. In this moment, although difficult, remember these emotions are a part of life. Be gentle with yourself and repeat the following:

"I forgive myself just as I would forgive a loved one."

Take a moment to recognize any positive changes you've made in the past month. How does it make you feel to reflect on how you've been consistent with these changes?

What kind of thoughts are in your mind when you first wake up? What are some positive thoughts you can include to start your day with deeper intention?

Affirmation

Say this aloud:

I love and appreciate myself as I am

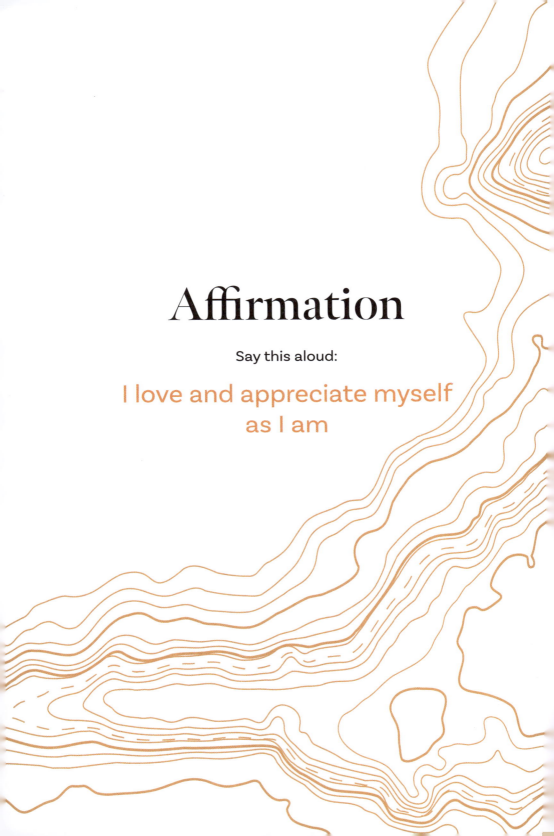

How can you show yourself more compassion?

What brings you a sense of peace? Reflect on how you can create more moments of peace in your daily life.

"

We say things to ourselves that we would never say to people we love

-Jay Shetty

Challenge Yourself

One day this week, be mindful of and eliminate any negative self-talk. Come back to this page and reflect on your challenges and wins for the day.

Was this an easy task? Why or why not?

What are your observations about your mood, your enviroment, your encounters, etc for the day?

Affirmation

Say this aloud:

I am consciously aware of and sensitive to the way I feel

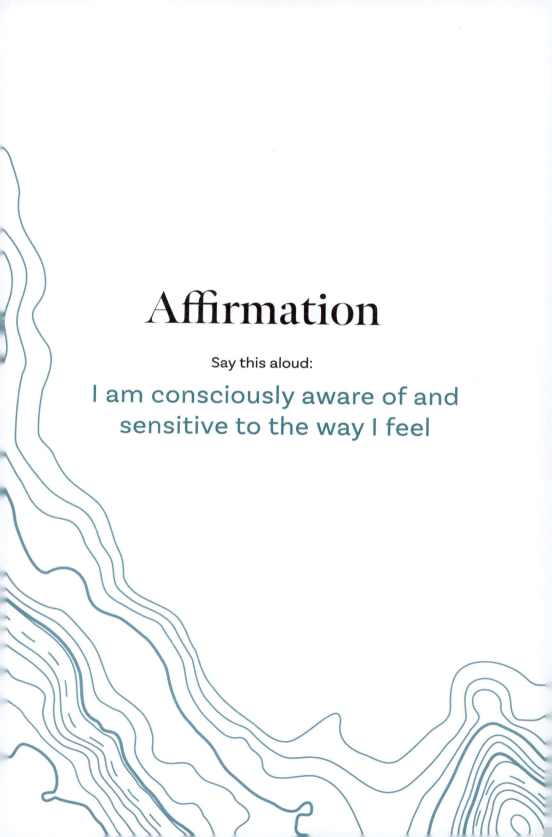

Remaining in the present moment is a key component of mindfulness. If you can be present, it is easier to remain positive. To do this, complete the following sentence: "In this moment I feel _____."

At this moment, how accepting are you of yourself? What would life look like if you fully accepted who you are?

What is your definition of self-love? How do you feel your interpretation of self-love plays a role in how you accept yourself?

Affirmation

Say this aloud:

I love myself unconditionally

Mindfulness Meditation

Loving-kindness

Find a quiet, private area and sit comfortably. Set a timer for 5 minutes. Place your hands over your heart's center while taking slow deep breaths. Breathe from your heart and allow yourself to feel deep, loving-kindness for yourself.

Repeat the phrase:
"I love you" silently or gently aloud until the timer goes off.

❝

You find peace not by rearranging the circumstances of your life, but by realizing who you are at the deepest level

-Eckhart Tolle

What brings you the most joy in life? Why does this bring you joy?

It has been shown that serving others can promote fulfillment and satisfaction. What are some of your favorite ways to give back to your community or the people in your life? How does giving to others promote a more positive mindset within you?

Write down 5 traits you love about yourself. Take a moment to celebrate yourself for these qualities.

Mindfulness Meditation

Body Scan

The goal of this meditation is to become aware of your body's state. To practice this meditation, you will pay close attention to physical sensations throughout your body.

Begin by focusing your attention on your feet. Become aware of any sensations such as pain, pressure, coolness, or warmth. Slowly carry your attention up your body to your calves, knees, thighs, pelvis, stomach, chest, back, shoulders, arms, hands, fingers, neck and lastly, your head. Once you reach your head, carry your attention once again back down through your body slowly. Remembering to only observe.

The goal is not to change or relax your body but just bring awareness to it. This meditation can be performed anywhere.

TherapistAid.com

Before going to sleep tonight, write down all the things you're grateful for. How does reflecting on gratitude make you feel?

Take a few moments to write an encouraging letter to yourself. Remember to use compassion. Reflect on this letter whenever you feel you need to hear these words.

Affirmation

Say this aloud:

I am positive and optimistic.
I believe things will always work out for the best

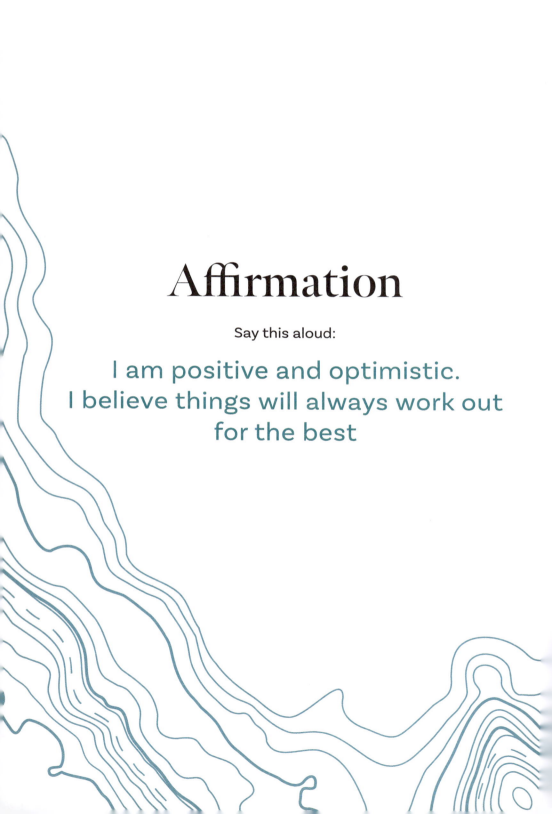

Reflect on a time when a circumstance did not work out in your favor but you learned a valuable lesson from the experience. Write down the details of this instance. How does this change your perspective on what's going on in your life right now?

_____
_____
_____
_____
_____
_____
_____
_____
_____
_____
_____
_____
_____
_____
_____
_____
_____
_____

Think of one very small action you can do to invite more positivity into your life. Over time, how can this one action lead to significant life changes?

> Your future is created by what you do today, not tomorrow

-Robert Kiyosaki

Challenge Yourself

For one day, choose to see the positive in every situation.

Take note of how your perception transforms the way you experience your day-to-day tasks.

Think about your current community. What is the most fulfilling part of your community? How does your community support your positive lifestyle?

One way to experience intense fulfillment is our ability to genuinely and graciously receive support. Do you truly allow yourself to receive support from others? Is there anything standing in your way of being able to receive support from the people around you?

We always attract into our lives whatever we think about the most, believe in most strongly, expect on the deepest levels, and/or imagine most vividly

-Shakti Gawain

Imagine your funeral. What legacy did you leave? What do you wish you had done? What do you regret not giving more attention to? What skills did you acquire that you cherished most?

How can you incorporate the desires and visions of yourself from the previous prompt into your life now?

The Self-work

The more you know and value yourself, the more authentically you can live

> Living a life of peace and purpose means having a clear picture of your identity and values

-Jay Shetty

Identity Wheel Exercise

- Take a look at this identity wheel.
- Circle the aspects of this identity wheel you feel comfortable with.
- Underline the aspects of this identity wheel you feel uncomfortable with.

Identity Wheel

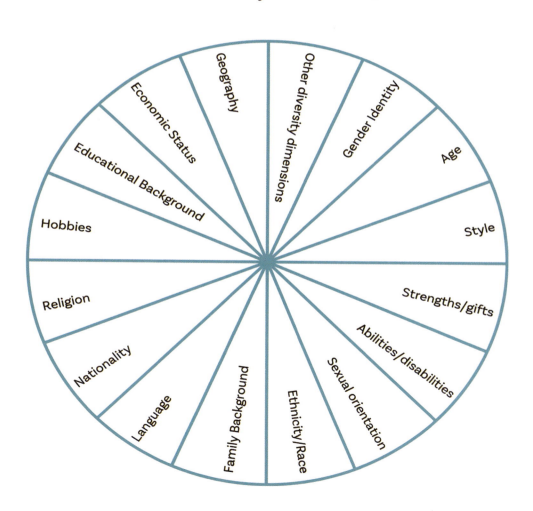

Why are you comfortable with the aspects you circled?

_____
_____
_____
_____
_____

Why are you uncomfortable with the aspects you underlined?

_____
_____
_____
_____
_____

How can you begin to acept parts of your identity you are uncomfortable with?

Tip of the Iceberg Exercise

The tip of the iceberg is only a fraction of what lies below the waterline. Icebergs can be analogous with how we perceive our identity.

Aspects of our outward facing identity, i.e, nationality, age, abilities/disabilities, etc only reflect a small portion of who we are and why.

In order to accept parts of ourselves that we sometimes reject, it is important to get to know ourselves on a deeper level.

Use the identity wheel from the previous exercise to write down 5 aspects on the top portion of the iceberg which can be found on the following page.

Reflect on what these aspects of your identity mean.

For instance, many people label me as socioeconomically disadvantaged, but what that means for me is that I am resourceful, I am creative, and I can make something from nothing.

Now write what your interpretation of these labels actually are for you underneath the water line.

Tip of the Iceberg Exercise

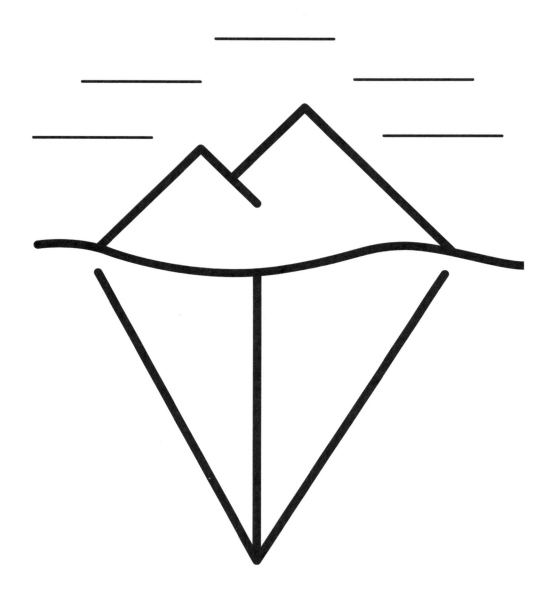

"

It is impossible to control conditions that others have created

-Esther Hicks

Identifying Triggers Exercise

Triggers can be defined as memories, objects, or people that spark intense negative emotions.

Here are a few examples of common triggering encounters:

passive-aggression
blaming
crying
criticism
entitlement
deceit
sarcasm
arrogance
etc.

After a triggering encounter, these are some common physical and emotional symptoms:

dizziness
chest pain
increased heart rate
nausea
shaking
anger
anxiety
sadness
fear
anger
frustration
etc

TherapistAid.com

Identifying Triggers Exercise

Identifying triggers will take time and requires self-awareness and introspection. However, you can begin to identify your triggers by paying close attention to your strong emotional and physical reactions after specific encounters or occurrences.

For instance:

Observation:
My supervisor doesn't encourage me as often as I feel I deserve.
Interpretation:
My supervisor does not appreciate my hard work.
Emotional response:
Frustrated, irritable, etc.

Observation:
My friend is always late to everything I plan.
Interpretation:
My friend does not value my time or effort
Emotional response:
Sadness, anger, etc.

Observation:
Someone raises their voice in a heated debate.
Interpretation:
This person does not respect me or my opinion.
Emotional/Physical response:
Anger, increased heart rate, shaking, etc.

TherapistAid.com

Identifying Triggers Exercise

Many times, our fight or flight response is activated so quickly to certain observations or stimuli that we are unable to stop the physical symptoms. However, with awareness of what is taking place we can develop our ability to manage how we respond. The next time you feel a physical or emotional reaction during an encounter try the following:

1. Ask yourself if you've been triggered.

2. Identify what thoughts and memories arise as a result of the observation.

3. Consider how you can respond to the current situation with this awareness.

You may also consider these questions:

Why do certain observations cause me to react so strongly?

What from my past is being reactivated as a result of this encounter?

TherapistAid.com

Core Values Exercise

The goal of this exercise is to define your core values in order to guide your decisions. With core values at the forefront, you will be able to prioritize what you feel is important when challenges arise.

1. Take a look at the following page for a list of values. Circle the ones that resonate with you.

2. Write these values down on the following page. Think abut the origin of these values. Are they from your family, the media, personal life experience, religion, intrinsic, etc.?

3. Once you have chosen your top 5 core values, rank them by priority. Whenever you are faced with difficult decisions rely on your core values to guide you.

List of Core Values

Authenticity	Justice
Achievement	Kindness
Adventure	Knowledge
Authority	Leadership
Autonomy	Learning
Balance	Love
Beauty	Loyalty
Boldness	Meaningful Work
Compassion	Openness
Challenge	Optimism
Citizenship	Peace
Community	Pleasure
Competency	Poise
Contribution	Popularity
Creativity	Recognition
Curiosity	Religion
Determination	Reputation
Fairness	Respect
Faith	Responsibility
Fame	Security
Friendships	Self-Respect
Fun	Service
Growth	Spirituality
Happiness	Stability
Honesty	Success
Humor	Status
Influence	Trust worthiness
Inner Harmony	Wealth

* Feel free to add additional values not found on this list

Value   Origin

My Top 5 Core Values

1. _____
2. _____
3. _____
4. _____
5. _____

* Bonus tip: Revisit your core values every 6 months. You'll be surprised how often they change!

Assessments

Following the core values exercise are a series of assessments to bring awareness to different aspects of your life.

Bringing awareness to each area of your life allows you to be more mindful about how you spend your time and your mental and emotional energy.

You cannot make adjustments if you do not have a baseline.

Use the folowing 3 exercises to create a baseline of awareness for yourself:

Habit Tracker
Money Assessment
Inner Circle Assessment

Habit Tracker Exercise

Evaluating your habits can increase your awareness about what you value. Tracking your daily habits also has the potential to hold you accountable for your actions and keep you on track to reach your goals.

For one week assess your habits using the habit tracker on the following page.

Observe the decisions you make.

Do your core values align with your current habits?

Week of :

Habit	Mon	Tue	Wed	Thu	Fri	Sat	Sun
	☐	☐	☐	☐	☐	☐	☐
	☐	☐	☐	☐	☐	☐	☐
	☐	☐	☐	☐	☐	☐	☐
	☐	☐	☐	☐	☐	☐	☐
	☐	☐	☐	☐	☐	☐	☐
	☐	☐	☐	☐	☐	☐	☐
	☐	☐	☐	☐	☐	☐	☐
	☐	☐	☐	☐	☐	☐	☐
	☐	☐	☐	☐	☐	☐	☐
	☐	☐	☐	☐	☐	☐	☐
	☐	☐	☐	☐	☐	☐	☐
	☐	☐	☐	☐	☐	☐	☐
	☐	☐	☐	☐	☐	☐	☐

The Self-Work

Do your core values align with your current habits? If not, what will you do so that your habits are reflective of your core values? What new habits can you adopt that reflect your core values?

Money Assessment

Evaluating your spending habits can also increase your awareness about what you value. Tracking your daily/monthly spending habits helps you mange your finances and keeps you on track to reach your financial goals.

For one week assess your spending using the expense sheet on the following page.

Observe how you spend your money.

Do your core values align with your highest spending category?

Week of: _____

Expenses

Date	Item	Amount

Overview

Category	Total	Category	Total
Savings			
Bills			
Food			
Entertainment/Fun			

Highest Spending Category: _____

The Self-Work

Does the category in which you spend the majority of your money reflect your core values? If not, what will you do so that how you spend your money is reflective of your core values?

Inner Circle Assessment

Evaluating your inner and outer circle could also bring awareness to what you value. Your inner circle has an impact on many aspects of your life. You can identitfy parts of you that are created or reinforced based on who you spend the most time with.

For one week write down every person you spend time with.

Tally up how many hours you spend with each person.

Based on total number of hours spent, place the people within the rings on the following page to define who makes up your inner circle.

Name	#of Hours

My Inner Circle

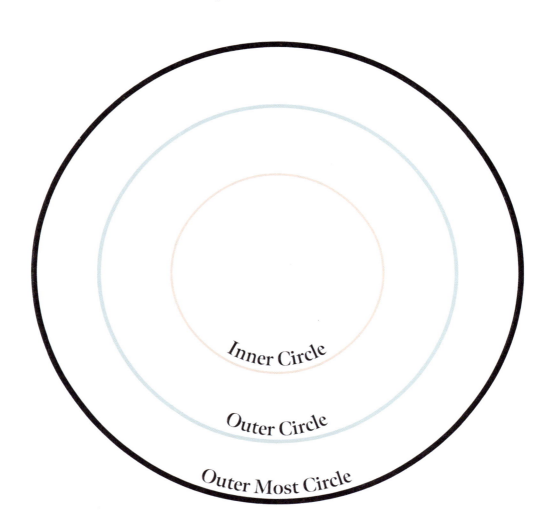

How do you feel about the people you spend the most time with?

_____
_____
_____
_____
_____

Is it important for the people in your inner circle to share your core values?

_____
_____
_____
_____
_____

❝

You will never change your life until you change something you do daily. The secret of your success is found in your daily routine

-Darren Hardy

Goal Setting Exercise

Opportunities are endless in graduate school. The outcome of this exercise is to clearly define your goals so they may guide which opportunities will be prioritized according to their alignment with what you truly desire.

1. Reflect on your core values from the previous exercise. How do these core values shape your goals?

2. Take a look at the following page and reflect on your goals in each of the indicated areas: health, self-care, personal development, career, home life, relationships, and finances.

3. Go through each of the following pages and make a list of your goals in each category.

4. Begin with identifying your long-term goals. Next identify intermediate and short-term goals that create momentum toward completing the long-term goal.

5. For each of the set of goals attribute a strong why for acheiving these goals

*Bonus Tip: After achieving a short term or intermediate term goal, reassess your long-term goals to see if they are still relevant.

Goal Categories

Self-Care

Nutrition
Introspective growth
Rest & Rejuvination
Work-life balance

Personal development

Mental
Emotional
Spiritual
Physical

Career

Skills/Techniques
Professional development
Network

Home-life

Physical Space
Organization
Atmosphere

Relationships

Family
Work
Romantic
Friendships

Financial

Income
Budgeting
Money management
Debt

Self-Care Goals

Long-term Goals

1.

2.

3.

Why:

Intermediate Goals

1.

2.

3.

Why:

Short-term Goals

1.

2.

3.

Why:

Personal Development Goals

Long-term Goals

1.
2.
3.

Why:

Intermediate Goals

1.
2.
3.

Why:

Short-term Goals

1.
2.
3.

Why:

Career Goals

Long-term Goals

1.
2.
3.

Why:

Intermediate Goals

1.
2.
3.

Why:

Short-term Goals

1.
2.
3.

Why:

Home-Life Goals

Long-term Goals

1.

2.

3.

Why:

Intermediate Goals

1.

2.

3.

Why:

Short-term Goals

1.

2.

3.

Why:

Relationship Goals

Long-term Goals

1.

2.

3.

Why:

Intermediate Goals

1.

2.

3.

Why:

Short-term Goals

1.

2.

3.

Why:

Financial Goals

Long-term Goals

1.

2.

3.

Why:

Intermediate Goals

1.

2.

3.

Why:

Short-term Goals

1.

2.

3.

Why:

Prioritization Exercise

Use the following table to help rank your goals. The left column ranks the priority of the goal category vertically. Then, beginning with the short-term goals rank their priority horizontally.

Goal Category	Goal #1	Goal #2	Goal #3	Goal #4
#1 Priority				
#2 Priority				
#3 Priority				
#4 Priority				
#5 Priority				
#6 Priority				
#7 Priority				

Visualization Exercise

Choose one long-term goal from the previous exercise. Visualize achieving this goal. How do you feel after it is accomplished? What kind of life are you living as a result of accomplishing this goal? What were the challenges you faced to achieve this goal?

Write a letter to yourself in congratulations for completing all of these goals and the growth you've experienced as a result of accomplishing them.

"

Self-discipline is the ability to do what you should do, when you should do it, regardless of how you feel

-Brian Tracy

Challenge Yourself

Write down your top 5 short term goals on separate sticky notes. Place these near a mirror to hold yourself accountable every day. Each time you accomplish a goal, remove the note and replace it with the next goal until you have accomplished the long term goal.

Self-limiting Beliefs

Self-limiting beliefs, otherwise known as cognitive distortions, are irrational thoughts that have the power to influence how you feel. This is completely normal; everyone has cognitive distortions to some degree. However, when cognitive distortions or self-limiting beliefs are too extreme or abundant, they can be harmful.

There are many types of cognitive distortions or self-limiting beliefs that may affect our ability to accomplish our goals, such as:

Polarized "All or Nothing" Thinking
Overgeneralization
Mental Filtering
Disqualifying the Positive
Mind Reading: Jumping to Conclusions
Magnification or Minimization
Emotional Reasoning
Should Statements
Labeling and Mislabeling
Personalization

Identify these thoughts within yourself and challenge them with a positive affirmation. In these moments, use self-compassion.

In one column write down some of the self-limiting beliefs you have that may hinder you from achieving these goals. In the other column, write down an affirmation you can replace these self-limiting beliefs with.

Self-limiting belief	Affirmation

Refer to the previous goal setting exercise and affirmations. What would accomplishing these goals look like if you believed the affirmations instead of your self-limiting beliefs?

"

It's not about controlling thoughts, it's about guiding thoughts

-Ester Hicks

My Character Exercise

Being intentional about shaping your character can help set clear boundaries about who you are and who you are not. Defining your character can also fuel the "why" behind your goals and your reasons for undergoing rigorous experiences such as pursuing a PhD. There is a list of character traits on the following page. Use this page to write down a maximum of 10 character traits of the person you need to become to accomplish your long-term goals. Conversely, write down 10 character traits that person you does not embody.

1) Reflect on your goals and your core values from the previous exercises. Think about the character of a person who has accomplished those goals and who possesses those core values.

2) Reflect on the character traits of a person who is unable to accomplish these goals to define who you are not.

3) The next time you are faced with a difficult task, think about the character trait(s) you are building through the challenge. Think about how developing this character trait will help you achieve your long-term goals.

List of Character Traits

Demanding
Thoughtful
Keen
Happy
Disagreeable
Simple
Fancy
Plain
Excited
Studious
Inventive
Creative
Thrilling
Intelligent
Proud
Fun-loving
Daring
Bright
Serious
Funny
Humorous
Sad

Lazy
Dreamer
Helpful
Simple-minded
Friendly
Adventurous
Timid
Shy
Pitiful
Cooperative
Lovable
Ambitious
Quiet
Curious
Reserved
Pleasing
Bossy
Witty
Energetic
Cheerful
Smart
Impulsive

Use this page to write down a maximum of 10 character traits of the person you need to become to accomplish your long-term goals. Inversely, write down 10 character traits that person does not embody.

Who I am becoming | Who I am not

Make a list of skills you have learned or need to learn pertaining to your degree. For each skill write a character trait that can be reinforced through performing or learning this skill. For instance, the skill, scientific writing is reinforced by the character trait of self-discipline.

Skill	Character trait

Think of a difficult situation you are faced with in your program. What character traits are being developed through this difficult situation? Does this align with the person you need to become to accomplish your long term goals, why or why not?

Affirmation

Say this aloud:

I cannot attract what I don't possess

Academic Perception

A strong sense of purpose and identity abrogates the conventional academic journey

Challenge Yourself

You are the Principal Investigator of a laboratory space. This lab space represents your mind, and the people who come and go represent your thoughts. Some lab members are excited and optimistic while others are pessimistic and draining. You can choose how you react to those lab members, just as you can choose to respond to critical thoughts.

Negative emotions and thoughts will inevitably arise throughout this journey, but you are the PI of your own mind.
How will you react?

Affirmation

Say this aloud:

Prioritizing my mental health and physical well-being is essential to my success as a graduate student

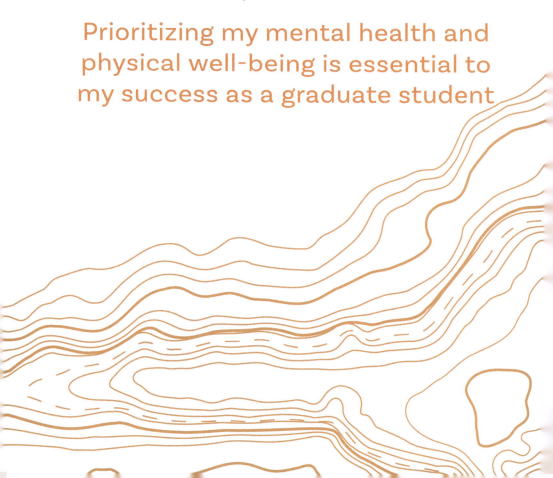

Reflect back to your life before beginning your graduate program. Write a list of all the reasons you decided to pursue graduate-level education.

Refer to the previous prompt, have the reasons you listed changed? If so, how have they changed and why have they changed?

Write a list of challenges you encountered throughout higher education that could have held you back from getting where you are today. Reflect on how far you've come.

_____
_____
_____
_____
_____
_____
_____
_____
_____
_____
_____
_____
_____
_____
_____
_____

Refer to the previous prompt, for each challenge write a positive character trait you gained through overcoming this challenge.

Challenge | Character Trait

Write about a time in a research environment when you felt you made a mistake. How did people around you respond? How did this make you feel? How do you wish they would have responded?

"

Inside every problem lies an opportunity

-Robert Kiyosaki

Reflect on one of your favorite, most supportive mentors. Write a letter about yourself from their perspective. List all the reasons they think you deserve to pursue graduate education. How does this make you feel?

Think about a recent challenge you overcame in an academic setting. Write about this challenge and acknowledge any feelings that arise. What lessons did you learn from this experience? How can this experience prepare you for future positions within your career?

Reflect on the last 72 hours. What is one thing you did that makes you proud? How does it feel to reflect on this?

Affirmation

Say this aloud:

Every time I step out of my comfort zone my confidence grows

Reflect on a difficult situation you encountered this month. Did you handle this situation like you wanted to? Why or why not?

Refer to the previous prompt. Write down as many positive outcomes as you can about this situation.

Are there any previous failures you think about as a student that prevent you from being in the present moment? If so, write them down.

Refer to the previous page. Cross out these failures. Give yourself permission to let go of these "failures." Now write about the version of yourself that is free from this instance.

"

Your true knowledge comes from
your own life experience

-Esther Hicks

Imposter Syndrome

Imposter syndrome refers to an internal belief that you are not as competent as people perceive you to be.

Signs you may be experiencing imposter syndrome include: self-doubt, overachieving, sabo-taging your own success, inability to assess your competence and skills, and attributing your success to external factors.

Perfectionism plays a huge role in imposter syndrome. To overcome this perfectionist mindset you may try the following:

1) Make a realistic assessment about your performance, abilities, and skills

2) Stop comparing yourself to others

3) Question the irrational thoughts that arise regarding your skills

4) Reassure yourself with affirmations

5) Accept your success and celebrate your wins

Positivepsychology.com

What did you do well today?

Who can you consistently count on to encourage you when you need support? How does it feel to have this person's support?

Affirmation

Say this aloud:

I deserve love and support

Challenge Yourself

When you feel Imposter syndrome creeping in, ask a trusted mentor a series of reflective questions to reassure yourself of the work you are doing and why you're qualified to do it. Examples could be similar to the following:

a) What are my greatest strengths?
b) How have I grown since you first met me?
c) How do you think I'm doing?

Reflect on all the graduate programs you considered. Why did you ultimately choose your program?

Currently, how accepting are you of your journey as a doctoral student? What would graduate school look like if you fully embraced where you are in your journey?

Affirmation

Say this aloud:

Regardless of the circumstances, I deserve to be at peace

Describe the qualities of your ideal mentor and the resources within your lab environment and department/program. How do these absence or presence of these qualities effect your success as a graduate student?

Challenge Yourself

Reflect on the expectations you have of your mentor, your lab mates, and/or your department/program. Imagine approaching each of these entities with no expectations (like an empty cup), ready to receive. Reflect on all the qualities and resources these entities possess, outside of your personal expectations.

Express gratitude for what these entities have to offer you.

> Was it a bad day or was it a bad 5 minutes you allowed to disrupt your entire day?
>
> —Unknown

In a perfect academic world, every student would have unconditional support tailored to their individual needs. However, in most instances this is not the case. Take a moment to reflect on the support you receive from your cohort, your program/department, your mentor, administrative staff, previous mentors etc. Are you satisfied with it? If not, how can you supplement your support to help you thrive in this academic setting?

_____
_____
_____
_____
_____
_____
_____
_____
_____
_____
_____
_____
_____

Write down all of the things going well in your graduate program. How would your life be different if you focused on these things more?

Choose one good thing from the previous page. Write down all the ways in which your life would be different without this. Express gratitude for this good thing.

Write down a list of self-limiting beliefs specifically regarding your PhD journey. Similarly to the exercise on page 105, for each of these beliefs write an affirmation that you can replace this self-limiting belief with when it arises.

Self-limiting belief | Affirmation

In simple terms, the language you use to describe your circumstances determines how you see, experience, and participate in them and dramatically affects how you deal with your life and confront problems both big and small.

-Gary John Bishop

What did you accomplish in the last 48 hours pertaining to your degree or studies that you can give yourself a little more recognition for? How does it feel to give yourself a little extra credit?

Reflect on a time related to graduate school when you thought something would not work out in your favor and it did. How does this change your perception of what's going on right now in your graduate program?

What resources do you need to aid your success as a graduate student? This can range from lab supplies and expertise to community and support.

Burnout

Burnout can be defined as a state of emotional, physical, and mental exhaustion caused by excessive prolonged stress. Often this can be characterized by a number of symptoms. Here are a list of common symptoms and remedies to help you cope with burnout.

Symptoms

Physical: feeling drained, low energy, headaches, irregular sleep patterns

Emotional: low self-esteem, lack of motivation, feeling detached, persistent negative thoughts

Behavioral: isolating yourself, reduced performance at work, procrastinating more than usual, mood swings

Remedies

Physical: exercise, eat nutritious foods, get enough sleep, meditate, journal

Emotional: engage in mindfulness exercises, redefine your 'WHY,' practice self-compassion, use affirmations

Behavioral: surround yourself with supportive friends, take time off from work, prioritize what's most important

Positivepsychology.com

"

The only thing more contagious than a good attitude, is a bad one

-David Goggins

What you choose to focus on, you magnify. Write down three great things that have happened to you this week. Reflect on how these instances made you feel.

Write a list of everything you are grateful for as a graduate student. How can you express your gratitude more often in your daily routine?

Challenge Yourself

Often, we overlook our needs for more "urgent" situations that we feel need our attention more than we do. Take a moment to check in with yourself and your needs. Complete this sentence for as much as you need: "Right now I need_____."

Write about a time in higher education where you felt the most empowered/safe. What was your daily routine like? Who made up your friends' group? Describe your work environment. How did this make you feel?

Write down your most recent accomplishment in your program, it doesn't matter how big or how small. How did you feel after achieving this? Allow yourself to feel those feelings again. Remember this feeling when working toward your next goal or milestone.

_____
_____
_____
_____
_____
_____
_____
_____
_____
_____
_____
_____
_____
_____

"

Whether you think you can or you can't, you're right

-Henry Ford

When you celebrate the wins of others as if they were your own wins, you amplify the amount of joy you can experience. Reflect on the last couple months. Write down the accomplishments of friends, family, lab mates, and cohort mates. What emotions arise?

Affirmation

Say this aloud:

I am always, in all ways, growing confidently in the direction of my desires

Write down a list of all the things you're looking forward to within your PhD program. It doesn't matter if this is year one or year five. How does this make you feel?

Think of a close cohort-mate or mentor, how would they describe you as a graduate student from their perspective. Take a moment to savor these kind words.

Each day this week after finishing your experiments/tasks, write down all the skills you used, using this phrase, "I am grateful for _____ skill." How does reflecting on all your abilities make you feel?

Write down the negative thoughts that are causing you to doubt your ability and adequacy as a graduate student. Now, rewrite each thought as the inverse and affirm yourself by saying these words to aloud. For example, negative thought: "I don't belong in this program" Inverse/Affirmation: "I belong here."

Skill	Character trait

When you fail or make a mistake, what helps you grow back your confidence?

Affirmation

Say this aloud:

I completely and easily release all fear of failure

Graduate students often have a difficult time acknowledging their skills. What is something you're really good at? Take a few moments to brag about yourself!

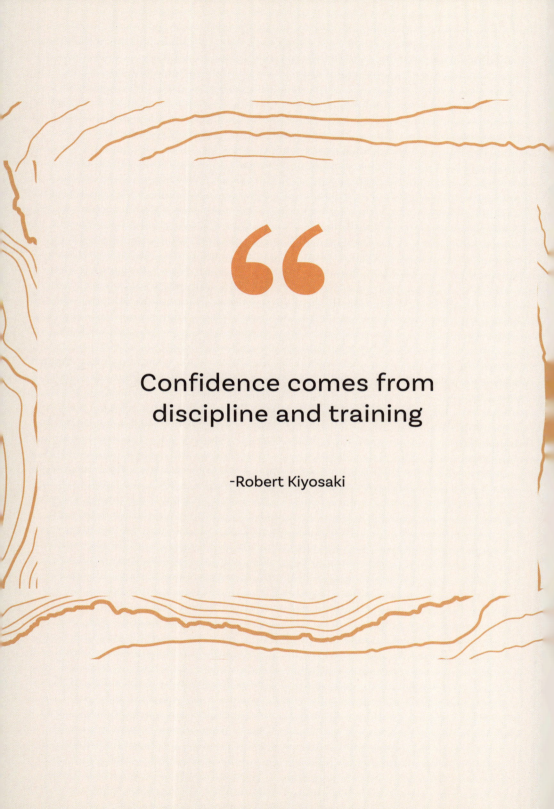

"

Confidence comes from
discipline and training

-Robert Kiyosaki

Challenge Yourself

Take some time to think about what you truly desire along your doctoral journey. The types of connections you want to make, experiences you want to have, the journals you want to publish in, defense day, mentors, friendships, job offers, etc. Find a magazine or google pictures of these items and print them out to create a vision board. Be open to allowing all of this into your journey.

Write about a time when you handled a situation in a way that reflected your values and goals. How did this make you feel?

What do you enjoy most about your graduate school journey right now? How does this promote a more positive outlook on your studies?

Inner Peace

Inner peace can be defined as a state of psychological or spiritual calm despite the presence of potential stressors. It is a homeostatic psychological state, which results in the optimal functioning of the mind.

There are many ways you can cultivate inner peace.
1) Spending time in nature
2) Meditation
3) Gratitude
4) Affirmations

The more you heal from past trauma and practice these methods, the more inner peace you will have. Cultivating a state of inner peace eliminates anxieties, fears, and worries and reduces negative thoughts, stress, dissatisfaction, and unhappiness.

Obtaining a state of inner peace will promote emotional and mental stability, happiness, confidence, and inner strength.

Comfort yourself in this moment.

Positivepsychology.com

Think of one very small boundary you can set and adhere to consistently to promote a more peaceful experience as a student. How could this small boundary contribute to more peace on a daily basis?

Affirmation

Say this aloud:

I do not worry about things that are not within my control

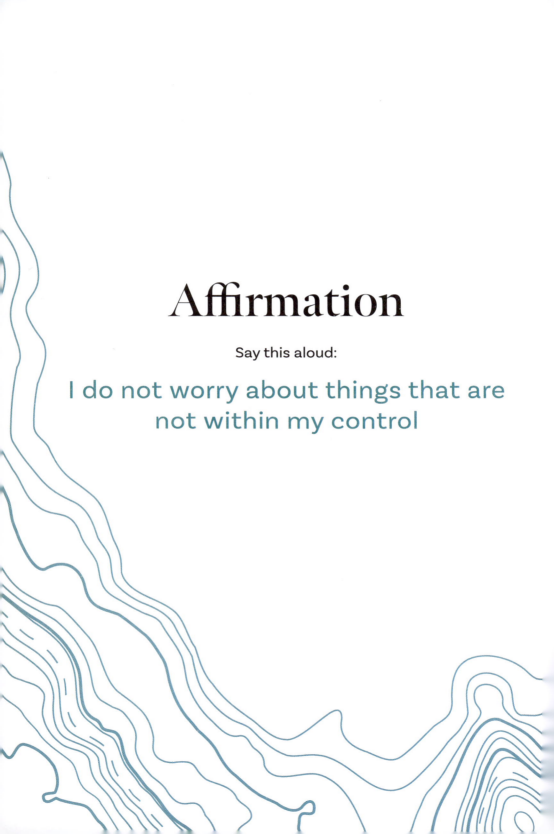

What part of your academic journey brings you the most joy? Why does this bring you joy?

_____
_____
_____
_____
_____
_____
_____
_____
_____
_____
_____
_____
_____
_____

What qualities do you want people to remember most about you as a graduate student? How would it make you feel to be remembered in these ways?

Imagine your thesis defense day. What legacy did you leave within your lab? What do you wish you had done? What experiences do you wish you had? What do you regret not giving more attention to? What skills did you acquire?

How has your perspective changed as a graduate student after reflecting more deeply about your identity and both your personal and academic journey? How does this make you feel?

Affirmation

Say this aloud:

My happiness does not depend on others. The happiness of others does not depend on me

Final Thoughts

It starts with you.

My world changed because I surrounded myself with supportive people, prioritized my well-being, and reflected deeply to find purpose in everything thing I do. The standard of "the academic" in the traditional sense is not my standard. I define what success looks like for me.

Your strengths as a doctoral student overlap with mindfulness practices: learning from mistakes, analyzing results in an unbiased way, inventing creative methods to solve problems, and understanding systems on an intimate level.

You can undoubtedly do the same on a personal level for yourself.

I truly believe that if each of us takes responsibility for our own happiness we can transform not only our experience as academics but the experience of those around us.

It is my hope that The Mindful PhD will resonate with doctoral students and reverberate through doctoral programs worldwide to change how we experience higher education for the better.

"It is not a lack of strength, not a lack of knowledge, but rather a lack of will."

Are you willing?

#TheMindfulPhD

Resources

I hope you have enjoyed the mindfulness exercises in this journal. Here are a few resources that I use to implement mindfulness practices in my daily routine:

Meditation Mixtape-shelahmarie.com/meditations: If you'd like to ease into a guided meditation, the meditation mixtape was my first intro to a guided meditation that laid a solid foundation for how to breathe and what to meditate on.

I am- Daily Affirmations on the App Store: If you're looking for new affirmations or consistent reminders to speak positively to yourself the I am app has daily affirmations to help you rewire your brain and change negative thought patterns.

Coloring Book for Me- on the App Store: If you're looking for a new way to de-stress, I recommend coloring. I use it to relax and allow my mind to wander.

MinimaList- To-Do List on the App Store: If you're looking for a simple way to keep track of tasks, I recommend the Minimalist. It's a simple to-do list, a reminder, a checklist, a task manager that helps you to get things done.

Audible- Audiobooks on the App Store: If you're interested in reading more personal growth/development books audible is a great way to grow on the go. With Audible I can read in my car, at the gym, or while walking my dog and I find it very efficient.

Additional Mindfulness Exercises- positivepsychology.com: If you're looking for new mindfulness exercises to deal with specific obstacles or want to switch up your routine, I use the Positive Psychology website for new ideas. It's a science-based online resource packed full of courses, techniques, tools, and tips to help you put positive psychology into practice **every day.**

Book Recomendations

Bishop, Gary John. Unfu*k Yourself. Harper Collins, 2017.

Chubb, Tanaaz. The Power of Positive Energy. Simon and Schuster, 2017.

Gandy, Debrena Jackson. All the Joy You Can Stand. Harmony, 2001.

Gawain, Shakti. The Creative Visualization Workbook: Use the Power of Your Imagination to Create What You Want in Your Life. Full Circle Pub., 2000.

Goggins, David. Can't Hurt Me. David Goggins, 2021.

Hardy, Darren. The Compound Effect. Vanguard Press, 2012.

Kornfield, Jack. The Wise Heart: A Guide to the Universal Teachings of Buddhist Psychology. Bantam Books, 2009.

Layne, Erica. The Minimalist Way. Althea Press, 2019.

Marie, Shelah. Positive You. Rockridge Press, 2021.

Meadows, Martin. How to Build Self-Discipline. Meadows Publishing, 2015.

Proctor, Bob. You Were Born Rich. 1984.

Shetty, Jay. Think Like a Monk. Simon & Schuster, 2020.

Tolle, Eckhart. The Power of Now: A Guide to Spiritual Enlightenment. Hachette Australia, 2018.

Tracy, Brian. No Excuses!: The Power of Self-Discipline. Hachette Go, 2020.

Walsch, Neale Donald. Conversations with God. 2010.

References

[1] Whitfield, T., Barnhofer, T., Acabchuk, R., Cohen, A., Lee, M., Schlosser, M., Arenaza-Urquijo, E. M., Böttcher, A., Britton, W., Coll-Padros, N., Collette, F., Chételat, G., Dautricourt, S., Demnitz-King, H., Dumais, T., Klimecki, O., Meiberth, D., Moulinet, I., Müller, T., … Marchant, N. L.. (2021). The Effect of Mindfulness-based Programs on Cognitive Function in Adults: A Systematic Review and Meta-analysis. Neuropsychology Review.

[2] Kabat-Zinn, J. (2003). Mindfulness-Based Interventions in Context: Past, Present, and Future. Clinical Psychology: Science and Practice,10(2), 144–156.

[3] Shapiro, S. L., Carlson, L. E., Astin, J. A., & Freedman, B. (2006). Mechanisms of mindfulness. Journal of Clinical Psychology,62(3), 373–386.

[4] Baminiwatta, A., & Solangaarachchi, I.. (2021). Trends and Developments in Mindfulness Research over 55 Years: A Bibliometric Analysis of Publications Indexed in Web of Science. Mindfulness, 12(9), 2099–2116

[5] Shapiro, S., & Weisbaum, E. (2020). History of mindfulness and psychology. Oxford University Press.

[6] Kabat-Zinn, J. (1994). Wherever you go, there you are: Mindfulness meditation in everyday life. New York: Hyperion.

[7] Hofmann, S. G., & Gómez, A. F.. (2017). Mindfulness-Based Interventions for Anxiety and Depression. Psychiatric Clinics of North America, 40(4), 739–749.

[8] Brown KW, Ryan RM. The benefits of being present: Mindfulness and its role in psychological well-being. J Pers Soc Psychol. 2003; 84(4):822-848. [PubMed: 12703651]

[9] Keng, S.-L., et al., Effects of mindfulness on psychological health: A review of empirical studies, Clinical Psychology Review (2011).

[10] Lillard, A. S.. (2011). Mindfulness Practices in Education: Montessori's Approach. Mindfulness, 2(2), 78-85.

[11] Shapiro, D.H. (1992). A preliminary study of long-term meditators: Goals, effects, religious orientation, cognitions. Journal of Transpersonal Psychology, 24(1), 23-39.

[12] Kabat-Zinn, Jon. Full Catastrophe Living: Using the Wisdom of Your Body and Mind to Face Stress, Pain, and Illness. New York: Bantam Books, 2013.

Acknowledgements

Thank you to my best friend, my angel, Kai Monique Penn who planted this seed of mindfulness within me. Thank you to my San Diego community and church family who have supported me unconditionally throughout my spiritual journey and academic career. To my community in Seattle, thank you for all of the love and support I received from you through an extremely difficult time. Thank you to my UNC-CH and North Carolina community for encouraging me and empowering me to share my journey. To the professionals, that helped me put this journal together and launch my platform, thank you. I express my deepest gratitude to my mother who has been my biggest cheerleader since birth, thank you for all your unconditional love and support.